I HAVE AN ALCOHOLIC PARENT.

NOW WHAT?

TERRY TEAGUE MEYER

ROSEN
PUBLISHING®

New York

Published in 2015 by The Rosen Publishing Group, Inc.
29 East 21st Street, New York, NY 10010

Copyright © 2015 by The Rosen Publishing Group, Inc.

First Edition

Library of Congress Cataloging-in-Publication Data

Meyer, Terry Teague.
I have an alcoholic parent. Now what?/Terry Teague
Meyer.—First edition.
        pages cm.—(Teen life 411)
Includes bibliographical references and index.
ISBN 978-1-4777-7982-8 (library bound)
1. Alcoholics—Family relationships—Juvenile literature.
2. Children of alcoholics—Juvenile literature. 3. Alcoholism—Juvenile literature. I. Title.
HV5132.M493 2015
362.292'3—dc23
                                                    2014009014

Manufactured in China

CONTENTS

Courtney was in her teens before she figured out the connection between alcohol and the constant storm raging at her house. When she visited with friends, she often found herself envious of their relationships with their parents. At home, she and her brothers and sisters had to be on their best behavior all the time. They never knew what mood their parents would be in—happy or angry. Those moods were extreme and could change in an instant. Dinners and barbeques at friends' houses didn't start with drinks and end with people yelling at one another. Finally, Courtney realized that her parents were alcoholics. They couldn't control their drinking, or what happened once they started.

Courtney is not alone. The 2012 National Survey on Drug Use and Health found that 6.5 percent of the American population reported

Children of problem drinkers never know when the next family fight will break out. Their parents' behavior is hard to predict.

heavy drinking in the past year. That's seventeen million people. The results were the same in 2011. Worse, people between the ages of twenty-six and fifty had even higher rates of heavy alcohol use. Between 7.1 and 9.9 percent of this age group drink heavily. This survey is based on reported usage, so it is very likely that many heavy drinkers underestimated or underreported how much they actually drank.

Many of these problem drinkers do not see themselves as alcoholics. Despite this, each one is well on the way to having serious health, work, or relationship problems because of drinking. Each of these heavy drinkers also has friends or a family or both who will be negatively affected by the excessive alcohol use. If you are aware—or beginning to suspect—that your parent (or parents) is an alcoholic, you probably feel alone and uncertain about what to do. This resource aims to provide information to help cope with this kind of situation.

First, it's important to know how experts define the many forms of alcohol abuse. Then its variety of causes can be identified. Doing both can help someone put a name to the problem at home. Being aware of available resources to help alcoholics and their families will help support those dealing with this situation. Learning about the different treatment choices available to aid recovery from alcohol addiction can offer hope.

All individuals and families are unique. Problem drinkers are also unique. Each has his or her own reasons, patterns, and behaviors associated with alcohol abuse. For this reason, an alcoholic's path to recovery must be an individual one. Fortunately, there are many treatment choices available. Family members impacted by a parent's addiction will also follow an individual path. Each one is affected according to his or her personality and position in the family. Whether or not the parent seeks treatment, the loved ones of an alcoholic must each find his or her own way to break free from the unhealthy environment created by addiction. That journey begins with understanding what lies ahead.

Experts recognize that all alcoholics are not alike. Even someone who does not fit the definition of "alcoholic" can still have a drinking problem. In turn, drinking problems threaten drinkers' health, work life, and relationships. Consequently, scientists and medical experts in alcohol use and abuse have a number of different ways to identify those at risk of alcohol abuse. One measure of how much is too much starts with understanding what a drink is.

WHAT'S IN THAT DRINK?

Each year, the Substance Abuse and Mental Health Services Administration (SAMHSA) conducts a National Survey on Drug Use and Health. It tracks alcohol

Many people don't know what it means to drink in moderation. It is important to understand how much alcohol is in any beverage you consume.

use and abuse around the country by age, gender, and race or ethnic group, among other categories. This study defines a drink as "a can or bottle of beer, a glass of wine or a wine cooler, a shot of liquor, or a mixed drink with liquor in it." The Centers for Disease Control and Prevention (CDC) gives a more specific definition of a drink. It is anything that contains 14 grams or 1.2 ounces of pure alcohol. So what does that amount look like?

- 12 ounces (1 ½ cups) of beer or wine cooler.
- 8 ounces (1 cup) of malt liquor. Malt liquor looks like beer, but has a higher alcohol content.
- 5 ounces (a little more than 1/4 cup) of wine.
- 1.5 ounces (3 tablespoons) of distilled liquor like whiskey, gin, rum, or vodka. This kind of alcohol is often called hard liquor.

It's important to know what a drink is. The problem is that many problem drinkers might be unaware of what makes a drink. Some drinkers ignore the problem saying they drink "only beer" or "only wine." However, they might consume as much alcohol during an evening as someone drinking hard liquor. Wine, distilled liquor, and mixed drinks can be particularly difficult for problem drinkers. They can easily fool themselves into thinking that a cocktail or wine glass filled to the brim is one drink, when it might actually contain up to four servings of alcohol.

Experts at the CDC and elsewhere define moderate drinking as one drink a day for a woman and two drinks a day for a man. This difference has to do with size. A man's larger size allows him to metabolize, or process, more alcohol than a woman, as women on the average tend to be smaller. Moderate drinking means one or two drinks a day; it does not mean seven drinks on Saturday night after not drinking all week. According to the CDC, binge drinking is defined as four or more drinks during a single occasion for women and five or more drinks for men. More than one or two drinks per day is considered heavy drinking. Binge drinking is another type of alcohol abuse.

No Alcohol Allowed

For some people, alcohol is particularly dangerous and no amount can be considered safe. A pregnant woman could harm her unborn child by drinking. The National Council on Alcoholism and Drug Dependence (NCADD) reminds pregnant women that when they drink, the fetus is directly affected by the alcohol. Unborn children can suffer a range of disabilities, from mild to severe. If a woman drinks very early in a pregnancy, even before she knows she is pregnant, there is even greater risk. For this reason, women planning to become pregnant or those having unprotected sex should not drink alcohol.

People under the age of twenty-one are not allowed to drink by law. Teens are inexperienced drivers. They often engage in risky behavior. Add alcohol, and the risk for auto accidents, fights, and sexual assault becomes much greater. Besides these risks, underage drinking is

particularly dangerous to health. The adolescent brain is still developing. Teens are therefore at greater risk than adults of becoming addicted to alcohol and drugs.

Prescription medication and alcohol do not mix. Alcohol can make many medications dangerous or less effective. The combination of drugs and alcohol can even be fatal. Even popular over-the-counter medications like acetaminophen (which is in Tylenol) can pose a health risk when combined with alcohol. Alcohol also increases risks for other health conditions, such as breast cancer and high blood pressure. Many alcoholics also die prematurely due to liver damage from alcohol.

No one should drink before driving, but people do. According to the National Highway Traffic Safety Administration (NHTSA), more than ten thousand people died in alcohol-related traffic accidents in 2010. That's one person every fifty-one minutes.

There are a number of ways to define problem drinking. According to the National Institute on Alcohol Abuse and Alcoholism (NIAAA), alcoholism or alcohol dependence is a disease. It is characterized by four common symptoms. (1) The person craves alcohol. (2) The alcoholic can't control drinking once he or she starts. That means one drink leads to too many others. (3) The person is dependent on alcohol. Stopping drinking produces physical and emotional

Pregnant women, or those hoping to become pregnant, should avoid all alcohol in order to protect a fetus.

YOU DON'T WANT A HIGH SCORE ON THIS TEST

The National Council on Alcoholism and Drug Dependence (NCADD) has created an online self-test for those worried that they have a problem with alcohol. Other organizations have similar tests available online. Having your parent take such a test would be helpful in getting him or her to recognize if alcohol use has gotten out of hand. The test below includes some questions similar to the NCADD self-test. The actual test is about twice as long. It is worded as a self-test, but you can use it based on your observations of the parent you suspect is an alcoholic. All questions can be answered yes or no.

1. Do you drink heavily when you are under pressure or upset?
2. Can you handle more alcohol now than you did when you first started drinking?
3. Do you sometimes have trouble remembering what happened the night before?
4. Has someone close to you expressed concern or complained about your drinking?
5. Do you often want to go on drinking after others say they've had enough?
6. Do you usually have a reason to explain times when you drink heavily?
7. When you're sober, do you sometimes feel sorry about things you said or did while drinking?
8. Have you tried switching drinks or following different plans to control drinking?
9. Have you broken promises made about quitting or reducing drinking?
10. Do you try to avoid family members or close friends when you are drinking?

11. Are you having more financial, work, or family problems because of drinking?
12. Have you gone to anyone for help about drinking?
13. Have any of your blood relatives had a problem with alcohol?

Any "yes" response to this self-test indicates an individual is at great risk of alcohol dependence. The scoring section of the actual NCADD test indicates that a score above two "yes" answers is cause for concern. The organization recommends that anyone scoring above eight should seek counseling for a more detailed assessment.

withdrawal symptoms like upset stomach and anxiety. (4) The problem drinker needs to consume more and more alcohol in order to get a pleasurable feeling. This is because he or she now has a tolerance for alcohol and a smaller amount will no longer produce a high, or a good feeling. Depending on the drinker, sometimes the good feeling never comes.

Just because someone doesn't show all the symptoms listed by the NIAAA doesn't mean he or she doesn't have a very serious problem. Alcohol abuse is a pattern of drinking that results in harm to a person's health, interpersonal relationships, or ability to work. The terms "alcohol dependence," "alcohol addiction," and "alcoholism" can be used interchangeably. However, whatever the term, the condition is characterized by a person's craving for alcohol and inability to limit drinking. These terms will all be used to describe problem

Children of alcoholics may not realize that the problems they experience at home are caused by alcohol abuse. They may consider family drama and chaos normal.

drinking. Drinkers themselves might be unable to recognize when they have a problem, but those close to them usually do.

Recognizing an Alcoholic in Your Own Home

How a person behaves might show alcohol dependence. He might make bad choices. He or she might try to drive after drinking too much. Or he might have lost a job because of poor performance or not showing up at work. After drinking, parents might say mean and nasty things. They could become physically violent. In some families, the signs of alcohol abuse are

easy to spot. In others, that is not always the case. Some children and teens who grow up with an alcoholic might not know that all families are not like theirs. As they grew older, these children might begin to notice that other families are different. Their friends' parents might be more attentive, more often present, or less moody than their own. An adult child of two alcoholic parents reports that she didn't realize the difference in families until her teen years. She had no idea that other families were not in a constant state of turmoil. As children, she and her siblings only knew that they had to be very careful around their mother. No one could ever predict how their mother would act or what would make her lash out in anger.

In the family of an alcoholic, routine but important things often get neglected. Regular meals, attending school events, or picking children up from practice can go undone. At the same time, the alcoholic parent might focus attention on unimportant things. Kids might feel parents become upset and lay blame for no apparent reason. Children whose parents are becoming alcohol dependent right before their eyes might notice a gradual change in a parent's behavior. For example, a parent who lost a job might give up looking for a new one after a while and spend the day "doing nothing."

Personality also plays a role. A person's personal situation and pattern of drinking all affect behavior. Some people become lively and sociable under the influence of alcohol. Others might become withdrawn. There are so-called "happy drunks" and "mean drunks." A single individual might go from lively to unpleasant to violent in a single evening. A parent might simply disappear for a time and come home after the children are in bed. He or she might simply fall asleep in front of the television while having another drink.

It is helpful to know what a drink is and what experts define as too much, as described above. Then it might be easy to tell if a parent is drinking too much. Other signs of excessive drinking are slurred speech and the loss of motor function. Typically, police test whether people are sober enough to drive by having them do simple tests. Police might ask a person suspected of intoxication to walk a straight line. Standing on one leg is another typical test. Counting backwards is another. At home, observing whether a parent stumbles upstairs to bed or has trouble using the television remote can show if he or she is drunk. A parent who smells of alcohol or is unable to help with homework might have had too much to drink.

LET'S NOT TALK ABOUT IT

The myths on page 22 are typical of a long list of explanations, excuses, and complete lies used to cover up a serious alcohol problem. Psychologists call this being in a state of denial. The person in denial believes that refusing to recognize a problem will make it disappear. The alcoholic can easily convince himself that he is in

Changes in behavior can show that a person had too much to drink. Excessive alcohol can make it hard to walk, talk, or perform simple tasks.

control. After all, the problem drinker's mind is under the influence of a drug. However, it is very common for the families of alcoholics to be in denial, as well. Some parents might try to hide a drinking problem from the family by drinking alone or away from home. Even though a person might have an obvious problem, his family might ignore it. A child growing up with an alcoholic parent might find it hard to discuss the problem with others in the family. It is very common for families of alcoholics to work hard at keeping the problem a secret.

Why would whole families choose not to talk about this serious problem? According to family therapist Mary Branson (see page 38), the family members see their situation as normal. They want the comfort of feeling that they are just like everyone else. Members of families affected by alcoholism often fall into certain roles. This makes it possible for the family to appear to be operating as smoothly as any other.

Myths and Facts about Alcoholism

MYTH

I don't have an alcohol problem. I only drink beer.

FACT

Beer, wine coolers, or hard liquor—the delivery system doesn't matter. Anyone who regularly drinks more than one or two drinks a day likely has an alcohol problem.

MYTH

My dad isn't an alcoholic. He has a good job, with no problems at work.

FACT

Many people are so-called functioning alcoholics, meaning they manage to do what's needed to hold down jobs and carry out normal duties. They might drink only after work but still manage to regularly consume enough alcohol to cause health and relationship problems.

MYTH

I can stop drinking any time I want.

FACT

This kind of statement is an example of how alcohol abusers deny having a problem. The drinking patterns of people who make this claim often show that they are only fooling themselves. They frequently stop drinking only to start again.

CHAPTER 2

What makes it possible for some people to drink in moderation while others can't stop? The medical community, social scientists, and mental health professionals have studied the problem. They conclude that it's very complex. There are many factors that contribute to alcoholism. It is almost impossible to identify a single cause, even in the same individual. The most common factors are discussed below. However, it's important to recognize that factors often work together to lead to a drinking problem.

IT RUNS IN THE FAMILY

People inherit certain traits from their parents. They might share a tendency toward high cholesterol, cancer, or diabetes. Likewise, alcoholism seems to run in families. For those with a strong family susceptibility to alcohol, a first drink might lead to immediate problems. This was the case with Marlon Farley. His family's struggle with alcoholism was profiled in a video entitled "Coping with an Alcoholic Parent." Marlon's parents were both alcoholics. His childhood was spent basically raising himself and taking care of his parents. When he took his first drink as

a teen, he says he knew he was in trouble. Still, for many years, he was unable to avoid following the family pattern of alcohol abuse. In a publication entitled "A Family History of Alcoholism. Are You at Risk?" the NIAAA reports that studies show "children of alcoholics are about four times more likely than the general population to develop alcohol problems." This same article notes that more than one-half of all children of alcoholics do not become alcoholics. Still, the risks are considerable. Young people with a history of alcoholism in the family should think hard before ever trying alcohol.

ALCOHOL AS A "SOCIAL LUBRICANT"

Oil lubricates a car or machine to keep it running smoothly. Some say that alcohol keeps parties running smoothly, too. People use it to relax at social gatherings. Alcohol is common at celebrations. Shy people might drink to feel more at ease in a crowd. The term "the life of the party" refers to people who are funny and entertaining at social events. However, some of these people might be acting this way because of alcohol. Alcohol can release inhibitions. That means wild behavior might not be kept in check. Many people drink with friends

Often several different physical, mental, and social factors work together to lead to problem drinking.

Alcohol is common at social celebrations and everyday get-togethers. But many "social drinkers" don't know how to stop drinking.

to unwind after a day at work. A person's friends might all be drinking buddies. But what starts as social drinking can still lead to problems. Those who become dependent on alcohol might start drinking long before a party starts. Excessive drinking at parties and family gatherings is often featured on television and movies. In real life, it can lead to permanent disruptions in family relationships, violence, and police action. If a parent's behavior at parties and social gatherings embarrasses members of the family, it might be a sign that his or her alcohol use is beyond control.

For the recovering alcoholic struggling to remain sober, social

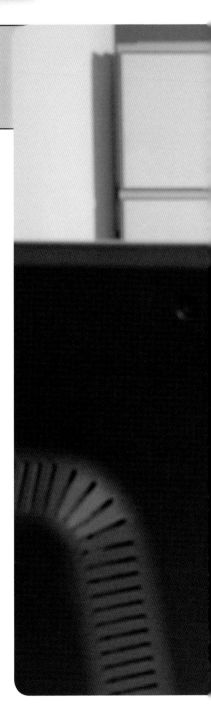

Alcoholism is often accompanied by mental conditions like depression and stress disorder.

situations are hard to handle. The sight of others drinking alcohol often sets off a need to join them. Habits like drinking at a bar after work might be too dangerous for the recovering alcoholic to risk. As a result, he might have to find new friends and new social outlets to avoid returning to drinking.

PSYCHOLOGICAL CAUSES

Substance abuse of all kinds is often associated with different mental conditions. These can be depression, severe mood swings, or problems expressing emotions. These conditions, which substance abuse counselor Jeff Jay

Is Alcoholism a Disease or Not?

For years, heavy drinking was considered a character flaw resulting from lack of will. More recently, it has come to be seen as a chronic disease. It is long lasting and difficult to cure, much like diabetes. However, many alcoholics still feel shame. This contributes to the difficulty people have in admitting they or someone in the family is an alcoholic. On the other hand, it is helpful for problem drinkers to see their disease as the enemy rather than to identify themselves as alcoholic and nothing more. The same is true for their families. An alcoholic is a flawed parent, but still a loved one.

Alcoholism is a disease. However, the alcoholic is responsible for trying to change. As family therapist Mary Branson points out, alcoholism is a progressive and ultimately fatal disease. It should be treated as early as possible. Millions of people have learned to control their alcoholism. Recovery might last years or a lifetime, but it is possible.

terms "co-occurring disorders," feed off each other. They often make a situation worse. Does the problem drinker use alcohol to cheer up when feeling depressed, or is he depressed because of alcohol abuse? Many people turn to alcohol to relieve the everyday stresses of work, relationships, and family life. Alcohol, after all, is a way to relax and forget things. But for too many people, unwinding with alcohol leads to addiction.

An alcoholic might not recognize how big his psychological problems because of drinking are. He might understand it only after becoming sober. In addition, many people use other drugs like cocaine or marijuana along with alcohol. Perhaps a tolerance for alcohol makes them seek another source for the high they once only got from alcohol. Certainly, the effect of alcohol on the brain's center of judgment leads people to take risks. These risks might include easily giving in to peer pressure. Sorting out how to treat alcoholism along with its associated problems begins with a thorough assessment. A professional needs to look at the individual's mental condition and pattern of substance abuse. The key to successful recovery is to treat other drug and mental problems along with the alcoholism. However, in many cases underlying conditions go undiagnosed or untreated. This might make it less likely that the alcoholic will recover successfully.

IF ONLY THAT HADN'T HAPPENED

A death in the family, the loss of a job, a failed relationship—any such life-changing event or combination of events can push someone into problem drinking. Such situations are called trigger events. They set off a certain chain of actions and reactions. For example, a nondrinking person with a genetic tendency toward alcoholism might take a first drink after a painful romantic breakup. Someone who used to drink only with friends after work might begin drinking alone after losing a job. Heavy drinking can bring about changes in brain chemistry that lead to addiction. So the individual who sought a

The stress of a life-changing event can sometimes lead people to start drinking heavily.

"solution" in drinking might find that alcohol has become the problem long after the trigger event.

IT'S ALL IN YOUR HEAD

Studies in brain chemistry show that alcohol and other drugs act on pleasure centers in the brain. Katherine Eban, an investigative reporter who specializes in the effect of drugs on the brain, describes how drugs produce a surge in the level of the neurotransmitter dopamine. "Neuro" means relating to the nervous center of the brain. "Transmitter" means something that sends out a signal. Eban notes, "When we experience something good... our brain experiences a surge in the level of the neurotransmitter dopamine. We feel warm, calm, and happy."

Neurotransmitters are the chemical substances that act as the body's communication system. It is not surprising that people enjoy the effect of dopamine and want to repeat it. Eban describes this process as the brain's "go system." It should be controlled by a "stop system" in the brain's prefrontal cortex. However, substance abuse disrupts this balance and allows the go system to run on its own. Nerve and brain patterns become habits. With overuse, the drug's pleasurable effect on the user decreases over time. This varies depending on the user's age, gender, and other individual factors. Still seeking the "buzz" (or good feeling) felt in the past, an individual might drink more and more to get the pleasurable effect. Eventually, the user no longer feels any pleasure but is unable to stop drinking.

The book *Addiction: Why Can't They Just Stop?* is a companion to the HBO video series. It includes information about how brain-imaging techniques have affected the medical community's view of addiction. CAT (computerized axial tomography) scans, MRI (magnetic resonance imaging) and PET (positron emission tomography) images have made it possible for scientists to view the effects of drugs and alcohol on living brains. This book contains information and actual scans of both normal and addicted brains. The differences are obvious. Such images answer the question, "Why can't they just stop?" The answer: addicted brains have changed in important and long-lasting ways. Consuming alcohol has become a top priority, no matter what the consequences.

CHAPTER 3

Problem drinking affects the whole family. Even in families in which functioning alcoholics hold down jobs and provide for their families and where there is no family violence, children and spouses are negatively impacted. To a large extent, alcohol abuse is a family disease. It affects everyone in some way. A genetic predisposition means that children of alcoholics are more likely to become substance abusers themselves. But even those who never take a drink are strongly influenced by growing up with an alcoholic. The effects of alcoholism follow children into adulthood. It can strongly influence how they behave in relationships, in their work life, and as parents.

Alcohol disrupts the normal balance of brain chemistry. Likewise, it disturbs the normal pattern of family relationships. Often roles are reversed. The alcoholic parent becomes more like a child who needs care and protection. The child might have to take on the role of parent. Those who disapprove of the alcohol abuse might still encourage or enable it, even as they try to help the situation. Family members might assume different roles and behave— either positively or negatively—according to those roles. Of course, all families of alcoholics are different, but certain patterns of behavior

Can you spot the alcoholic? Social situations that include alcohol create challenges for those trying to control their drinking.

are typical. Recognizing these roles in the family can help children of alcoholics break the pattern that enables their alcoholic parent.

ROLES PEOPLE PLAY

Psychologist and addiction expert Claudia Black and others have identified several roles that children of alcoholics and other substance abusers typically adopt. Counselors might give these roles different names, but the roles are recognizable in any family.

The Enabler

The alcoholic parent is not a fully functioning member of the family. This means someone else has to take on extra duties,

A Survivor Working to Help Others

Licensed professional counselor Mary Branson has practiced as a marriage and family therapist in the Houston, Texas, area for seventeen years. She counsels individuals and families dealing with problem drinking on a daily basis. She felt called to this profession because she grew up with an alcoholic father but did not understand until she was an adult how much alcohol affects the family as a whole.

Branson said she never recalled a time during her childhood when her father was not drinking heavily. He was a functioning alcoholic who was able to continue working. Outwardly, theirs was a model, happy family. But to keep up appearances, the parents and four children maintained a code of silence. They never admitted, even among themselves, that there was a serious problem. In this situation, each person took on a certain role. This is typical in families of addicts. The mother took over many responsibilities of the father. She was aided in this by the oldest child, who became a sort of other parent to the younger siblings. Other children assumed typical roles as the troublemaker, the clown, and the invisible child.

After the children had grown up and left home, the father stopped drinking by joining Alcoholics Anonymous. But his problem drinking already had lasting effects on his family. While none of the children became alcoholics themselves, three of them married alcoholics and the fourth had to overcome a substance abuse problem.

In her practice, Branson stresses the importance for children of alcohol abusers to seek counseling as early as possible. Spouses and children of alcoholics need to learn how being in an alcoholic family has affected them personally. She wants them to understand that growing

Alcoholism affects the whole family. Family therapy
is needed to deal with problems that can last a
lifetime.

up thinking an alcoholic family is normal can lead to
problems into the next generation. Even when the alcoholic becomes sober, there is a long road to recovery
for everyone involved.

When one parent drinks, often the other parent has to work harder to keep the family running. Sometimes this role even falls on an older child.

usually the spouse. For example, if Dad comes home from work and starts drinking, Mom would have to take care of meals, children's evening activities, homework help, and bedtimes. If Mom goes on a binge every weekend, Dad would have to cover weekend sports practices and errands. Often, the spouse steps in to take on extra duties, with the purpose of keeping the family running as smoothly as possible. He or she might be aided by an older child, the "hero," as defined below. Where both parents have a drinking problem, huge responsibilities fall onto older children.

An enabler is called this because he or she makes it

possible for the family to function "normally" while allowing the drinker to continue abusing alcohol. The enabler has good intentions. He or she might not see any other way to protect the family from the alcoholic's neglect. But enabling often makes the problem worse. By taking over tasks the alcoholic should be doing, the enabler makes it possible for the alcoholic to continue drinking. The alcoholic doesn't have to bear the full weight of the consequences of his or her behavior. Since someone else is making sure bills are paid and food is on the table, the addict can assume that everything is all right. Addicts are experts at ignoring problems and denying they exist, so it doesn't take much to enable one to continue drinking.

The Hero

This is the responsible child who tries to ensure that the family looks "normal" to outsiders. The hero might take on many responsibilities that the alcoholic parent neglects while still being successful in school and elsewhere. The hero seems to handle everything with ease, but the role is very stressful. Heroes don't have time to think about their own emotional needs.

The Scapegoat

A scapegoat is someone or something that takes the blame for what another has done. The scapegoat child

Children of alcholics may try to excel at everything while taking on extra responsibilities at home.

is the one who gets into trouble. He or she might do poorly at school or experiment with drugs and alcohol. In the alcoholic family, the scapegoat is the one who acts out, often in anger. The scapegoat's role in the family structure is to draw attention away from the bigger problem—the alcoholic parent.

The Mascot

The mascot, often the youngest child, is the entertainer in the family. This role also serves to focus attention away from the family's underlying problem.

Adjusters and Lost Children

Many children in alcoholic families seem to get lost in the chaos. They try not to make waves or focus attention on themselves. They act as peacemakers and do whatever they can to avoid creating family problems. Like other children in alcoholic families, these individuals ignore their own needs as they try to get along with others at home, no matter how difficult the situation.

None of the roles mentioned above leave much room for a kid to be a kid. The children of alcoholics are burdened by extra responsibilities, emotional neglect, and the need to adjust to unpredictable and often extreme situations. They are forced to become what one family therapist terms "pretzel children," tying themselves in knots in service to the family. At the same time, many are forced into silence about the family secret of addiction. The children of alcoholics get cheated out of good parental role models and a childhood that should be a carefree time of growth and experimentation.

FAMILY FALLOUT

The short-term effects of alcohol abuse can be terrifying. Drunkenness often leads to arguments. This might end in domestic violence and marital problems. When an alcoholic loses a job over poor performance, the loss of income can lead to hunger and homelessness. Failure to attend to basic finances like paying rent can also have devastating consequences. Drinking and driving is extremely dangerous, often fatal. If alcohol-related behavior puts someone at risk, it should be reported to a school counselor or other advisor who can connect with appropriate agencies and resources.

Since many family members of alcoholics don't want to talk about the problem, seeking help can be difficult. But doing so might be the only way to bring an end to domestic violence and neglect. Also, breaking the family code of silence is an important first step in dealing with the problem, just by recognizing and stating that it is a problem.

If you are experiencing this problem, allow yourself to express thoughts and feelings that might have been hidden for a long time. This is something helpful that you can do for yourself.

Lasting Effects on Children

Sadly, children of alcoholics often become alcoholics themselves. Many others marry alcoholics. Because they have grown up in a dysfunctional family that they considered normal, they are likely to model their lives on the family in which they grew up. The roles that children often adopt in response to substance abuse do not leave room for their needs to be met. Childhood and adolescence is a time of tremendous social and emotional growth and development. Much of this growth is nurtured and encouraged by a parent/child relationship that includes give and take. However, when the addicted parent neglects the needs of others, the children are left to raise themselves. Important steps in development get passed over. This often sets up the child for problems later in life.

The Adult Children of Alcoholics World Service Organization, Inc., exists to help those plagued by problems resulting from growing up with an alcoholic parent. The organization's website includes a statement of "the Problem" of children of addicts: "We lived life from the standpoint of victims. To protect ourselves, we became people-pleasers, even though we lost our own identities in the process." The website also features "the Laundry List" of fourteen characteristics of adult children of

Children of alcoholics are more likely than other people to become abusers of alcohol or other substances.

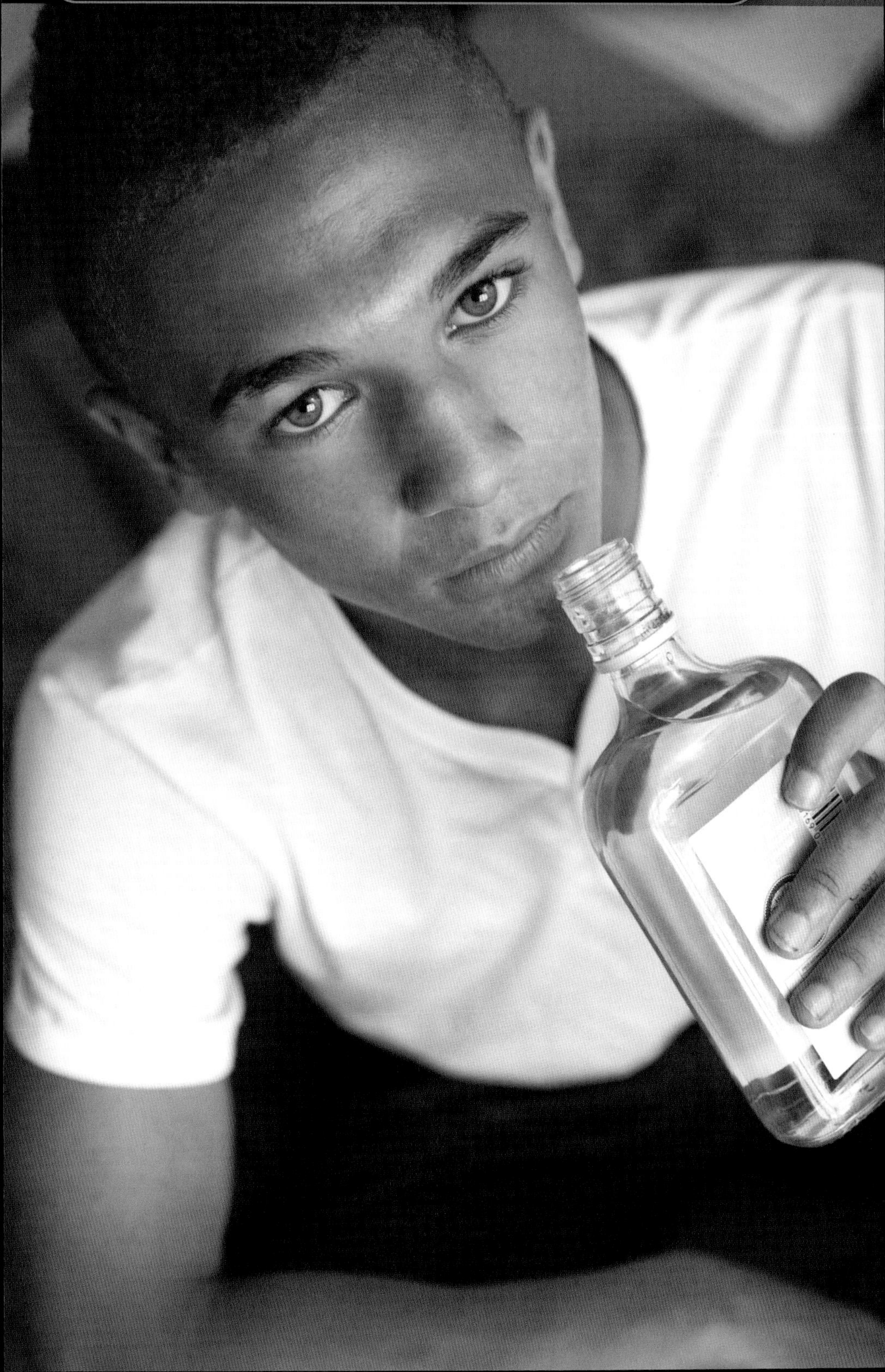

alcoholics. Among the traits are low self-esteem, problems dealing with criticism and authority figures, and a tendency to get into relationships with people who need to be rescued. "The Problem" and "the Laundry List" show a dreary future for those who have grown up with alcoholics.

In her classic book on children of alcoholics, *It Will Never Happen to Me*, Claudia Black shows how often children of alcoholics follow in their parents' paths. Dr. Black and many other therapists and substance abuse counselors emphasize that children of alcoholics should do everything they can to get treatment for themselves as early as possible. Too often, families suffer while focusing on trying to save the alcoholic parent or waiting for the addict to seek help. The children need help, too.

CHAPTER 4

Whether or not they are aware of it, family members of alcoholics develop coping mechanisms. Simply put, these are ways to deal with the situation. An individual's way of dealing with an addict depends on his or her personality and the behavior of the problem drinker. Is the addicted family member physically or verbally abusive, or merely absent and unresponsive to the needs of his or her loved ones?

How Families Cope

Denying that a problem exists is perhaps the major way individuals and families deal with a family addict. Family members might know or suspect what would explain an alcoholic's behavior, but they refuse to talk about it. . . perhaps hoping that the problem will just go away. More likely, they are fearful that those outside the family will look down on them once the family secret gets out.

The typical roles assumed by children of alcoholics give clues about how people cope. The hero helps out at home, often taking on adult responsibilities. At the same time, he or she strives to excel at school, in sports, and in other activities. Such positive outlets are healthy in many respects, but there is a downside. The

effort to hold things together at home and still shine elsewhere takes a tremendous toll on the individual. There is no time for negative thoughts, no opportunity to deal with the doubts, fears, and challenges that are part of growing up. The hero is pushed into the role of an adult early on, and the natural pace of maturing is disrupted.

Unhealthy—but common—responses among children of alcoholics include acting out in school, withdrawing from family and friends, and engaging in risky behavior. That might include substance abuse, smoking, cutting, sexual activity, and running away. None of these will help the situation at home, and they can have life-long negative consequences for the young person. Any child of an alcoholic might act out in one of these ways to try to get attention or to express anger and frustration. These kinds of behavior can be expected of the family scapegoat.

Some children of alcoholics react to the family situation by working harder. Some react by getting into trouble. Others, like the "lost child," try to adapt and just get along no matter what happens. Each is reacting to the environment created by an addicted parent. No matter what role they play in the addicted family, children share certain attitudes and behaviors that directly result from how they are treated. These are just a few examples:

The stress of life in an alchoholic family makes it hard for a kid to handle his or her own problems.

Lack of Trust

The alcoholic parent repeatedly breaks promises. She forgets school pickup time or doesn't show up for games or the school play. The parent might be unable to drive when it's time for soccer practice. After a while, the child stops counting on her or expecting her to do what she says. Some repeatedly break the biggest promise of all— to stop drinking. It's no wonder family members stop trusting her.

Hiding Feelings

Children often have trouble expressing unpleasant feelings. In the family of an alcoholic, some or all family members might be in denial. No one asks questions or expresses feelings that would naturally come up. Questions like, "Why is Dad angry all the time?" or "Why does Mom sleep so much?" or "Why do we never know if or when we'll have dinner?" do not get a response. When questions are asked and get no real answers, people stop saying what they are thinking. A problem drinker is not very sensitive to the needs of others. He might be emotionally or physically absent. When children of alcoholics have problems at school or break up with a girlfriend or boyfriend they need to be able to turn to an adult. If a parent isn't listening or is too drunk

Children of alcoholics learn they can't trust parents to carry out duties or keep promises.

The "invisible child" in an alcoholic family tries to avoid conflict by hiding feelings and keeping quiet.

to care, kids might bottle up their feelings. Why bother trying to express difficult feelings when no one pays attention?

Not Feeling

In her article "Portrait of an Alcoholic Family," therapist Dr. Tian Dayton discusses how those growing up in an alcoholic family are trained to shut down their emotions. She states, "Walls go up and battle lines get drawn as family members silently collude to keep their ever-widening well of pain from surfacing, blaming it on anything but what's really going on." They are often subject to fear, even terror. It awakens a natural instinct to fight or run

away. If the family members are unable to do either one, after a time, they will shut down all feelings. This way they can avoid the pain of fear, rage, and help-lessness the situation causes. The individuals might shut down such feelings for a time, even a very long time. However, feelings often surface in the form of unwanted reactions such as explosive rage, acting out, or depression. Dr. Dayton notes, "Their emotions and behavior seesaw back and forth from zero to ten and ten to zero with no speed bumps in between. They have trouble self regulating and living within a range of four, five and six."

In the case of a parent who is violent or verbally abusive, children learn to keep quiet and keep out of the way for their own safety. It might feel safe to do so but it is a form of enabling. If an individual in the family is at risk of harm from an alcohol abuser, someone should be notified as soon as possible. The risk of harm could be in the form of driving while drunk. A school counselor or other trusted adult is a good source of help. Help can also be found directly by searching online for "Child Protective Services" or "Child Abuse Hotline."

The coping strategies mentioned so far won't solve the problem of living with an alcoholic parent. Role play-ing and keeping silent are different forms of avoiding the issue while letting the alcoholic control the family. Strange as it might seem, the best way to deal with alco-holism in the family is to step back from the problem and concentrate on one's self. The situation is similar to that in an airplane safety presentation. Passengers are told to put on their own oxygen mask before helping someone else. In the same way, family members must focus on saving themselves rather than responding to the needs of the problem drinker. A person can only change himself. The family's wishes and complaints can't accomplish much. The addict must make a personal decision to change.

Attending an Alateen meeting might seem scary for a first-timer. It might be easier to get information from the Alateen website. Excerpts from *Alateen Talk* include stories of teens who are dealing with an alcoholic parent. In the For More Information section at the back of this resource, there are websites listed to help problem drinkers and their families. Online information is free and anonymous, but it's a one-way street. Talking to a school counselor or a trusted teacher or coach makes it possible to let out some of the pain of dealing with the situation. Children of alcoholics might find it difficult to reveal the family secret to a school counselor or other trusted adult, but doing so is a first step toward breaking out of the alcoholic family system. People cannot be arrested for being problem drinkers unless they break the law.

Turning inward to recognize and deal with your own feelings doesn't mean turning your back on the family or the alcoholic parent. Realistically, a substance abuser is the only one who can decide to stop drinking or using other drugs. Well-intentioned family members who take over the alcoholic's responsibilities while ignoring the

Help from Alateen

Alateen is an offshoot of Alcoholics Anonymous, specifically for teen children of alcoholics. Alcoholics Anonymous, known as AA, is a worldwide organization devoted to helping alcoholics get sober and stay sober. The organization was founded in Ohio in 1935 by two alcoholics, Bill Wilson and Dr. Bob Smith. It has since grown and is estimated to have more than 64,000 groups including 1.38 million members in the United States and Canada as of January 2013. At that time, the organization was estimated to have well over 114,000 groups and more than 2 million members worldwide. Due to the anonymous nature of AA, these figures are estimates. AA is free and supported only through voluntary donations. It is a mutual aid society, meaning that the members themselves support one another in their struggle against addiction. The AA "Twelve Step" program has become a basis and model for many addiction-recovery programs. Other programs to help people addicted to drugs, gambling, and overeating follow AA's model.

Two offshoots, Al-Anon and Alateen were created to help families and those in relationships with alcoholics. These groups are especially important since many alcoholics do not seek treatment. Dealing with their loved one's addiction is an ongoing problem for family members. Even family members with their own drinking problem still need support. Recovery is a long-term process. It often stirs up emotional and relationship problems that have been hidden for a long time. The most important aspect of Alateen is the opportunity it offers teens to speak frankly about their family situations. It is also beneficial to hear the stories of others who share similar experiences.

Substance abuse counselor Jeff Jay explains a typical Al-Anon meeting by pointing out that the organization "is about you, not the alcoholic." The idea is to help the family member find support and detach from the alcoholic's problems. As expressed in the AA book *The 12-Steps Unplugged,* the advice to family members is "live and let live." This means that family members should concentrate on getting on with their own lives, rather than focusing on the alcoholic. Alateen has its own Twelve Steps and Twelve Traditions adapted from those of the AA parent organization. The Twelve Steps of Alateen begin with the admission that "we were powerless over alcohol—that our lives had become unmanageable" and ends with a promise to help others in the same situation. In this case, admitting that one is powerless over alcohol means admitting that no one else can control an alcoholic's behavior. This statement is an important first step in detaching from another's problem to focus on one's self.

basic problem actually make it easier for the alcoholic to continuing drinking. Because of the close bond between parents and children, some children of alcoholics see themselves as part of the problem. Did that low grade on my test upset Mom? Would stop drinking and attend games if I made it to the varsity team? The answer to such questions is no. The SAMHSA brochure, which describes the basics of addiction treatment, provides good reminders for the families of addicts: "You did not cause your family member's substance use disorder. It is not your fault." The brochure adds, "Your loved one's recovery, sobriety, or abstinences does not depend on

Family members should seek counseling for themselves rather than wait for the problem drinker to change.

you." The family of an alcoholic also needs treatment. The family can recover from the effects of the alcoholism even when the addict does not. Family members are in treatment for their own benefit, not for the benefit of the substance abuser. The key is to focus on your own well-being.

10 GREAT QUESTIONS TO ASK A COUNSELOR OR FAMILY THERAPIST

1. What can I do to make my parent stop drinking?

2. What should I do if my drunken parent becomes violent?

3. If I report my parent's behavior, will someone break up our family?

4. The situation at home is making me miserable. What can I do to feel better?

5. How can I help other family members cope with Mom or Dad's drinking?

6. How long does it take someone to recover from alcoholism?

7. My parent is sober, but I'm mad about what went on before. How do I deal with my feelings?

8. I'm afraid my parent will start drinking again. What can prevent a relapse?

9. Will I become an alcoholic, too?

10. How will my parent's addiction affect me in the future?

CHAPTER 5

Mom or Dad has decided to get treatment. That's great news, but it doesn't mean the drinking problem is solved. There's an old saying that "a journey of a thousand miles starts with the first step." The first step toward treatment and recovery is tremendously important, but there is still a long journey ahead.

THE JOURNEY TO RECOVERY

What lies ahead depends in part on how the decision to stop drinking has come about. What is the alcoholic's mental and physical condition? Don't forget the question of money and insurance to pay for treatment. Many factors determine the course of an addict's path to recovery.

The alcoholic who personally decides it's time to change is farther down the road to recovery than those who have it forced upon them. Some people realize how severe their alcohol problem is when a serious health problem is diagnosed. Others might face up to the problem following a driving-while-intoxicated arrest or loss of a job due to poor performance. Alcoholics Anonymous assumes that the journey to recovery begins when an addict "hits bottom" and realizes he or she has no

In an intervention, loved ones confront the alcoholic in an effort to jolt him or her into seeking treatment.

control over alcohol and that life has become unmanageable. However, change can begin before someone hits bottom.

One means of getting a problem drinker to treatment is an intervention. To intervene means to step in to change the course of events. In substance abuse terms, an intervention is an event. People in the alcoholic's life confront him or her about the gravity of the problem. It is a joint effort to get the alcoholic into treatment. As described by addiction experts Jeff and Debra Jay in their book *Love First: A Family's Guide to Intervention*, a successful intervention requires a great deal of planning. It also needs participation from a

number of people close to the substance abuser. These loved ones come together, armed with letters expressing love and concern, and confront the alcoholic about the addiction. Arrangements to begin treatment should already be in place. Needless to say, the problem drinker could still refuse treatment, but the shock of the intervention is often what is needed to start the process.

Someone who has been abusing alcohol for some time is likely to have a great deal of difficulty going cold turkey. This is the act of stopping drinking suddenly and without supervision. The addicted body needs to be cleansed of the substance as a first step in the treatment process. This process is called detoxification, or detox. This is because the substance has been acting like a poison in the body. During detox, the substance is withheld until the patient's bloodstream is clear of it. Detox is also called medically supervised withdrawal. Medical supervision might be necessary because of the possible side effects of withdrawal, which refers to the physical effects of suddenly stopping use of an addictive drug. The situation becomes even more complicated in the case of those who abuse prescription or other drugs along with alcohol. According to guidelines from the Center for Substance Abuse Treatment (CSAT), withdrawal from alcohol used with barbiturates can be very dangerous. Withdrawal from alcohol and substances like cocaine and methamphetamine can create very unpleasant symptoms. It can be like a very bad case of the flu. Sometimes drugs are used to reduce the suffering of withdrawal. This helps the patient stay with the treatment plan.

TREATMENT FACILITIES

In her book, *Beyond Rehab*, writer Anne Fletcher describes the many types of facilities where substance abusers might be treated. In all of these treatment facilities, patients are supervised and provided counseling, often in groups, to help them stay sober. The types of facilities are described here briefly.

Residential

The patient stays at a residential treatment facility around the clock for weeks or even months.

Outpatient

The patient lives at home while attending treatment programs in clinics (some associated with residential facilities) and hospitals. Some outpatient programs require daily participation, while others require attendance only a few times a week. So-called intensive outpatient treatment requires nine to twenty hours a week of program activities. Outpatient programs typically last from two months to a year.

Inpatient

Round-the-clock treatment is provided in special sections of hospitals and clinics. This treatment is typically reserved for patients with serious physical or mental problems. Inpatient treatment might be used only for the detox period of treatment. Following detox, the patient might get less intensive treatment elsewhere.

Therapeutic Communities and Sober Living Facilities

These are places where a former addict might live in a structured and supervised community while relearning how to live a sober life.

Individual Treatment

The patient receives one-on-one counseling from a mental health specialist trained to deal with addictions and substance abuse.

IN THE MEANTIME, WHAT HAPPENS TO THE FAMILY?

The child of an alcoholic probably won't have any control over where his or her parent gets treatment or the kind. Many treatment decisions depend on insurance coverage and how to pay for it. Of course, medical and family considerations are also important when developing an appropriate recovery plan.

A SAMHSA publication entitled "What Is Substance Abuse Treatment: A Booklet for Families," provides complete information about treatment. It includes the role of family members in the treatment process. The first step is an assessment of the patient's current

First Lady Betty Ford shared her struggle with alcoholism with the American public. She founded the Betty Ford Clinic to help others recover from substance abuse.

Things should begin to look up once the alcoholic parent starts treatment. But recovery is an ongoing process.

condition. Part of the assessment process is gathering information about the substance abuser. It will likely cover things like:

- Medical history
- Medical problems
- Mental/emotional problems
- The amount of alcohol he or she regularly consumes
- Any other drugs being used
- Family situation and needs
- Current living situation and environment
- Employment history, stability, problems, and needs
- Previous treatment experiences in treating the substance abuse

Family members are often called upon to help in the assessment process. Sometimes the

alcoholic might be unwilling or unable to provide all the information needed. The booklet emphasizes how important it is to "be honest—this is not the time to cover up our loved one's behavior. The counselor needs to get a full picture of the problem to plan and help implement the most effective treatment." The information gathered in the assessment will be used to help put together an appropriate recovery team and craft a recovery plan.

STEPS ON THE PATH TO RECOVERY

The recovery team might include people like medical doctors, psychologists, social workers, and specially trained substance abuse counselors. Often those who counsel alcoholics have direct experience with the problem. They might be former addicts or family members of addicts. A caseworker assigned to lead this team will meet with the patient and, often, the family to discuss a treatment plan. The treatment plan includes the evaluation of the current situation, the goals for treatment, and the means to achieve those goals.

Following the assessment it might be determined that the patient does not need supervised detoxification. The assessment might uncover related physical and mental health problems like diabetes or depression. Other problems might require medication or different kinds of therapy. A social worker might be needed to connect a family with resources like assistance with food and housing costs. This is an important consideration if the addict is the only source of income for the family. The treatment plan will be changed over time as the situation changes. For example, detoxification is often the first step in a treatment process. Once the alcoholic is sober, the focus will turn to what is needed to keep the recovery process on track.

The treatment plan is bound to include extensive counseling. At first, the emphasis will likely be on individual counseling. The counselor will try to get the patient to see the extent of his or her problem and motivate a change. This process can be quite difficult, as many alcoholics have been denying their problem for years. In addition, the addicted brain continues to seek pleasure in alcohol, even when drinking no longer provides any pleasure. If not in the beginning, group therapy will soon be an important part of the recovery process. In group therapy, addicts share their stories of struggle and learn how others are learning to live without alcohol. In addition, the patient will likely have assignments to complete. This might include reading materials or watching videos. Journaling and reflection are also often part of treatment.

Learning to live without alcohol is a major concern in any recovery plan. The patient's drinking habit is woven into the pattern of his or her life. Alcohol might be the only way the drinker knows to relax, to reward him- or herself, to deal with stress, or to socialize. Imagine alcohol as a certain color of thread in a plaid fabric. If one could rip out that color of thread, the fabric would be in tatters, with loose ends everywhere. Ongoing counseling

Counseling, either individually or in a group, is part of any alcohol recovery treatment.

is necessary to help the recovering alcohol tie up the loose ends in life by developing sober life skills. These skills are new ways to deal with the ups and downs of life without resorting to alcohol.

Participation in Alcoholics Anonymous or other twelve-step programs is often included in recovery plans. Since its origins, AA and its offshoots have spread worldwide and helped countless alcoholics and substance abusers remain clean and sober. According to AA, the first step in recovery is to hit bottom and determine that one's life is out of control because of alcohol. The second and third of the twelve steps deal with surrendering one's life to a higher power. Later steps have to do with taking inventory of one's life. This inventory includes the alcoholic listing his or her shortcomings and the people who have been harmed by the drinking problem. Making amends and owning up to one's wrongs is part of the process.

AA counselors all come from the ranks of those who have recovered in the program. New members are assigned a sponsor whom they can call upon for help in their struggle. Many recovery programs require attendance at AA meetings as part of a treatment plan. However, AA itself considers attendance voluntary. The program is also free. Since alcoholism is considered a lifelong disease, many people attend meetings for years, particularly in times of stress.

While AA is one of the oldest and best-known substance abuse programs, it is not the best choice for everyone. Some people are put off by the focus on God in the Twelve Steps, although AA emphasizes that the concept of God is up to the individual. Other people find fault with AA's emphasis on hitting bottom before seeking treatment and the abstinence-only policy of recovery. Abstinence means no alcohol ever. Gabrielle Glaser, the author of *Her Best-Kept Secret: Why Women Drink—and How They Can Regain Control*, raises some typical objections to AA's insistence on total abstinence. According to Glaser, "Research shows that many problem drinkers . . . could benefit from brief interventions and practical advice about how to set better limits and change their drinking by cutting back." For example, drugs and help from organizations like Moderation Management help many problem drinkers to control alcohol use.

Moderation Management is a free nonprofit support group for those who want to control their drinking. This group is one of many that exist to help problem drinkers. A number of support groups focus on helping certain types of people. Two examples are Women for Sobriety and LifeRing Secular Recovery (for those seeking a nonreligious orientation). There are also a number of faith-based resources to aid in recovery tailored to, for example, Christians, Jews, Muslims, and Buddhists. See the end of this resource for further information.

CHANGE YOUR MIND TO CHANGE YOUR BEHAVIOR

Ending alcohol abuse is both a physical and a mental process. The abuser needs to talk about the problem. Former addict Christopher Kennedy Lawford writes in his book *Recover to Live: Kick Any Habit, Manage Any Addiction* that he had always thought he was special and that his situation as a drug and alcohol abuser was unique. But when he went to his first twelve step meeting, he heard a stranger telling a story that sounded exactly like his own. He writes that going to that first meeting "ruined" his using drink and drugs. "Because once you know you're not that different from all the other folks struggling with

Can't You Just Cure It with a Pill?

It would be great if someone could just take a pill and be cured of alcohol dependence. While there are currently several medications that can help addicts, the problem is very complicated. In his book *Healing the Addicted Brain*, Dr. Harold Urschel explains how these drugs work.

Disulfiram (trade name: Antabuse) is taken daily and is designed to make the patient feel sick if he or she drinks alcohol while on the medication. Because people know they will have a bad reaction while taking this drug, they are more likely to remain abstinent.

Naltrexone (trade names ReVia and Vivitrol) is designed to reduce alcohol cravings by disrupting the brain's association between alcohol and pleasure. It is used before the addict drinks alcohol. Over time, the drug reduces cravings because the addict no longer gets the expected buzz from drinking. One form of naltrexone is a pill taken daily. Vivitrol, the newer form, is given as an injection and lasts for thirty days.

Acamprosate (Campral) This drug appears to normalize brain activity that has been affected by alcohol abuse. After four to six weeks, patients have fewer alcohol cravings and begin to feel calmer and less stressed. It has not been shown to be effective in people who have not stopped drinking.

None of the drugs used to treat alcohol dependence are a "magic pill" that makes it easy to quit. Each is only part of a treatment plan. Another important aspect of treatment is learning new ways to deal with life's problems and social situations. For that, some sort of talk therapy is standard.

addictions, and that there is a solution, you can't pretend otherwise."

Lawford's breakthrough at that first meeting marked the beginning of a very long struggle. He has a family history of alcoholism. Following his own recovery from addiction, he made recovery the focus of his writing and his life. Cognitive therapy is only one of the recovery tools mentioned in his book.

The word "cognition" describes the mental action or process of getting information through thought, experiences, and the senses. Cognitive therapy challenges one's negative thought patterns in order to change behavior. Dr. Ann Manzardo, who specializes in addiction research at the University of Kansas Medical Center, explains, "The therapist teaches the patient how to identify negative assumptions that the patient makes about self and others, and suggests ways to reframe problems and behaviors more realistically." Cognitive therapy is based on identifying errors in thinking. Then patients change how they talk to themselves and practice making positive self-statements. For example, an alcoholic who thinks, "I'm miserable, so I need a drink," might be reminded that alcohol is a cause of the misery. Patients might be encouraged to speak their thoughts aloud (in private) because doing so often shows that these thoughts are illogical.

During the course of treatment, the therapist will help the client come up with more positive self-statements, sometimes called "bumper stickers." One

CHRISTOPHER KENNEDY LAWFORD
Kick Any Habit, Manage Any Addiction
CHRISTOPHER KENNEDY LAWFORD
Your Self-Treatment Guide to Alcohol, Drugs, Eating Disorders, Gambling, Hoarding,

example is, "There is only today." These statements challenge the negative thoughts that tell the alcoholic to react. They help to break past behavior patterns. By substituting new ways of looking at situations, the therapist helps the patient create new paths in his or her brain. Cognitive therapy is more active than some talk therapies. It requires the patient to learn and rehearse new responses to new thinking patterns. The patient practices new and different ways to cope with daily situations without returning to alcohol. It is like learning a new language.

Christopher Kennedy Lawford overcame drug and alcohol addiction and has devoted his life to helping others do the same.

The treatment phase is still only one step in the recovery process. After detoxification, therapy, and even months of treatment, the patient is not magically cured. But he or she is undoubtedly changed in many ways. After being in a controlled environment, like a hospital or rehab facility, returning home might be challenging. In a controlled setting, there was no alcohol available. Back at home and work, the recovering addict is faced with challenges. Familiar situations might act as triggers and bring on cravings. To keep from falling back into old patterns, the person will need to call upon new coping skills learned during treatment. Participants in AA are assigned sponsors who have gone through similar difficulties. The treatment team should still be in place and aware that the next phase of recovery might be the hardest.

THE FAMILY ROLE DURING TREATMENT

The alcoholic's family is probably in total support of the addict's recovery. However, the family is no longer the same. Family roles and routines that might have developed around the parent's drinking patterns are no longer appropriate. In fact, family members often find

What if the alcoholic stops drinking during a period of time and then starts again? Returning to old behavior patterns is called relapse. This medical term is used when a patient gets better and then becomes sick again. Experts emphasize that relapses are common. Some people even consider relapses to be a part of the process. People often fall back into old patterns of behavior. However, a relapse is not the end. The alcoholic is not back where he or she was before treatment. Relapses are often brief. Soon, the person in treatment is back on track.

SAMHSA indicates that about half of those who enter substance abuse treatment for the first time continue to recover. What about the other half? Many will have to go through detox and begin a treatment program several times before succeeding. Alcoholism is a chronic disease. For many people, it takes a long time to develop. Logically then, it takes a long time to get it under control. Family members are not responsible for relapses. They also can't do anything to prevent them. For this reason, it's best for each person to continue focusing on his or her own welfare at this stressful time.

Relapse prevention is an important part of most alcoholism recovery programs. Individuals must learn to deal with the cravings and triggers that caused them to lose control of their alcohol use in the first place. For example, those who used alcohol as a stress reliever need to find new ways to deal with everyday stress. Writer Christopher Kennedy Lawford recommends tools like meditation and yoga. The writer, a former addict, notes, "Mindfulness is a wonderful tool when you're dealing with cravings or the triggers or the impulses; it can help you become less reactive."

THERE MIGHT BE SETBACKS

The danger of relapse—returning to old drinking patterns—is an ongoing challenge for the recovering alcoholic.

themselves more confused than ever by a parent who is in many ways different from before. Family members might want to help the recovering alcoholic but do not know how.

The family who was in denial about a parent's alcohol abuse is not used to talking about it. Now that the problem is out in the open, it might be just as hard to begin sharing feelings. Many of these will be negative feelings. Optimism about the future might be colored by feelings of fear. There might be anger and uncertainty about what will happen next. Family members once might have felt neglected by a parent who was off drinking. Now they might be disappointed to find that he or she is away at

Changing the pattern of behavior that has led to an addiction requires retraining how the addict's brain works.

meetings or therapy sessions that are needed to stay sober. Each person in the family has to change roles and learn how to help the recovery.

RETRAINING THE MIND

In his book entitled *You Are Not Your Brain: The 4-Step Solution for Changing Bad Habits, Ending Unhealthy Thinking, and Taking Control of Your Life*, research psychiatrist Jeffrey Schwartz discusses the idea of looking at one's thoughts. He encourages examining them and, if necessary, "reframing" them. For example, someone experiencing a craving for alcohol could be trained to

change her response to cravings. A person can learn to recognize the uncomfortable physical sensation of craving as something that will pass on its own. Then, rather than act on the craving by giving in to it, the individual can mentally classify it as something the conscious mind can choose to observe without taking any action. Dr. Schwartz is an expert on how the brain develops habits and addictions. He also understands how the brain can change these same patterns in the body's nervous system. The key to changing patterns is to develop new ones. First, an individual must become conscious of old, negative patterns. Then she can focus on changing them.

Dr. Schwartz's model helps both the families of alcoholics as well as recovering addicts. Experts consider alcoholism a family disease. It infects the alcoholic's loved ones even when they don't drink. An alcoholic parent molds his or her children's thinking and behavior in such a way that counselors can predict family roles adopted by children of alcoholics. Those familiar with this family disease can also foresee the kind of relationship and emotional problems children of alcoholics can expects as adults. The family roles and patterns that have developed over time need to be interrupted to make way for healthier behaviors and ways for family members to relate to one another.

Working as a Family

Family therapy is a good way to help those in the alcoholic's family. They learn to deal with the changes in their lives that result from the alcoholic's treatment. Such counseling can also shed light on issues that might have contributed to the original drinking problem. Ideally, family therapy begins once it seems clear that the problem drinker is seriously committed to continuing recovery. During the initial stages of treatment, the alcoholic might be too preoccupied with his or her physical condition to deal with the feelings of family members. He or she might be resisting the whole idea of treatment. Family members might not even be allowed to talk to the loved one in treatment. Their only communication might come through letters. In addition, relapse is most likely to occur in the first months of treatment. It is better to begin family therapy after it is clear that the patient is committed to change.

Of course, family members might have already sought counseling or support from a group like Al-Anon or Alateen long before the addict has begun treatment. It is good for family members to seek help for their own problems as early as possible. However, by definition, family therapy involves the whole family and needs to include the recovering alcoholic.

What Issues Are Likely to Come Up in Family Therapy?

To begin with, people need to start talking about their problems. The issues that they refused to discuss or denied existed need to be addressed. Once people start talking, feelings will emerge. They might have been kept

Family therapy is important because alcoholism affects every member of the family in different ways.

under wraps for a long time. Often they are confusing and conflicting. Abused children will have to confront feelings of fear and anger. Those who have carried extra responsibilities on behalf of the underfunctioning parent might now express anger. Though they never complained in the past, therapy helps them understand the weight of that stress. The wife of alcoholic Marlon Farley, profiled in the video "Coping with an Alcoholic Parent," learned that what she thought was the best way to protect her family actually had a negative impact. She had been enabling her husband's drinking. The oldest daughter in the family had conflicting feelings. She said she was angry about having to act like an adult before she was ready. At the same time, she felt anger about losing her adult position in the family.

Family therapy brings members together in the same session with a counselor. The process can be painful. It might bring up unpleasant memories and bring out conflicts that seemed easier to just ignore in the past. The addict has to deal with physical discomfort that comes from cravings and withdrawal. So too, family members must face the pain of recognizing and changing negative behavior patterns created by a parent's addiction. In such sessions, people can learn to express themselves and really communicate with one another. They might even be doing that for the first time. Family sessions might uncover the need for additional individual or group counseling for some members of the family.

Even if the alcoholic relapses and fails to continue with the recovery process, the family should continue therapy. Each member must learn new ways to cope with a situation not of his or her own making. Literature supplied by the Adult Children of Alcoholics Society shows how important it is for family members to deal with problems stemming from alcohol abuse in the family as early as possible. Otherwise, the effects of alcoholism in the family continue into adulthood. It can even spill into the next generation.

GLOSSARY

abstinence The fact or practice of restraining oneself from doing or enjoying something (like alcohol or other drugs). Abstinence means not drinking at all.

addiction The condition of being physically or mentally dependent on something and unable to stop using it without negative effects.

assessment evaluation At the beginning of an alcohol treatment program, medical and substance abuse experts will make an assessment of the problem drinker's condition and situation.

chronic Refers to a condition, disease, or problem that is long lasting and difficult to cure.

cognitive therapy A type of psychotherapy in which negative patterns of thought are challenged in order to change unwanted behaviors or mood disorders.

craving A powerful desire for something. A craving for alcohol is a symptom of addiction and a challenge for the recovering alcoholic.

denial Refusal to recognize or acknowledge painful truths (like the extent of someone's problem with alcohol).

depression A mental condition in which a person remains very unhappy, without energy or interest in normal activities, over a long period of time.

detoxification (detox) Medical treatment or period during which a substance abuser does not use the drug, allowing the bloodstream to be cleared of the substance.

domestic violence Physical violence directed at a family member or someone who lives in the same home.

enabling Actions or behavior by others that might make it easier for someone to escape the natural consequences of his or her substance abuse.

genetic predisposition An inherited tendency to suffer from a certain condition or act in a certain way.

intervention Action taken to interrupt a pattern of events and change its outcome. Interventions are used to make addicts aware of a serious problem and get them into treatment.

physiologic Relating to the body and physical health.

psychological Relating to the mind and mental health.

recovery The return to a normal state of mind or health.

rehabilitation (rehab) Restoring someone to health or normal life by training and therapy. "Rehab" can refer to the process or the place where it takes place.

relapse A return to a worse state of health or behavior after a period of improvement.

sober A sober person has not been drinking alcohol. Sobriety is a continuing state of not using alcohol.

sponsor A member of AA who has been abstinent from alcohol for a long period and is ready to support a new member throughout his or her recovery.

stress Mental, physical, or emotional pressure.

substance abuse Using alcohol or other drugs in a way that harms the user and/or others.

therapy Treatment intended to relieve or heal a physical or mental disorder.

tolerance A condition in which higher doses of alcohol or drugs are needed to produce the same effect they had at first.

trigger An event or situation that causes something to happen or changes one's behavior.

withdrawal symptoms Physical changes occurring when a person stops or suddenly decreases alcohol or drug use.

FOR MORE INFORMATION

Adult Children of Alcoholics World Service Organization, Inc.

ACA WSO

P.O. Box 3216

Torrance, CA 90510

(562) 595-7831

Web site: http://adultchildren.org

ACA is a self-help, self-supporting organization that brings together adult children of alcoholics to discuss their common problems. The organization relies on the traditions and ideas of Alcoholics Anonymous.

Al-Anon Family Groups

1600 Corporate Landing Parkway

Virginia Beach, VA 23454

(757) 563-1600

Website: http://www.al-anon.alateen.org

Al-Anon and Alateen Family Groups meet worldwide to offer support and fellowship to children, spouses, and close friends of people with alcohol problems. The service is free and available to the family, even if the alcoholic is not seeking treatment.

Centre for Addiction and Mental Health (CAMH)

100l Queen Street West

Toronto, ON, M6J 1H4

Canada

(416) 535-8501

Website: http://www.camh.ca

CAMH is a research center and Canada's largest mental health and addiction teaching hospital. It provides clinical care, research, and education.

Mothers Against Drunk Driving (MADD)

511 E. John Carpenter Freeway, Suite 700

Irving, TX 75062

(877) 275-6233

Web site: http://www.madd.org

MADD is a national nonprofit organization that seeks to stop drunk driving and underage drinking. It supports victims of drunk driving and works to promote stricter alcohol policy. It is a good source of educational information on these topics.

National Council on Alcoholism and Drug Dependence (NCADD)

217 Broadway, Suite 712

New York, NY 10007

(212) 269-7797

Website: http://www.ncadd.org

This organization provides information about preventing and recovering from drug and alcohol abuse. Through local affiliates, it provides treatment and support for recovery from addiction.

National Institute on Alcohol Abuse and Alcoholism (NIAAA)

5635 Fishers Lane, MSC 9304

Bethesda, MD 20892

(301) 443-3860
Website: http://www.niaaa.nih.gov
This is one of the twenty-seven centers of the U.S. National Institutes of Health. The NIAAA is dedicated to conducting research on the effects of alcohol on human health and well-being. The website provides useful information about the effects of alcohol abuse.

Ontario Ministry of Health and Long-Term Care
M-1B114, Macdonald Block
900 Bay Street
Toronto, ON M7A 1N3
Canada
(866) 534-3161
Website: http://www.health.gov.on.ca
This Ontario ministry, like those in other Canadian provinces, serves the health needs of those who live there. The ministry's services include those related to mental health and addiction treatment and prevention.

Research Society on Alcoholism
7801 North Lamar Boulevard, Suite D-89
Austin, TX 78752-1038
(512) 454-0022
Website: http://www.rsoa.org
This professional organization provides a meeting place where scientists studying alcoholism and the effects of alcohol can exchange ideas. The society is also involved in education and government policy related to alcohol.

Secular Organizations for Sobriety (SOS)
P.O. Box 741

Amherst, NY 14226
(716) 636-4869
Website: http://www.cfiwest.org/sos/index.htm

SOS, which also stands for "Save Our Selves," is a mutual support society for those recovering from problem drinking. Is it an alternative to Alcoholics Anonymous in that it does not emphasize God or a "higher power." The organization provides a database with information about local meetings.

Substance Abuse and Mental Health Services Administration (SAMHSA)

1 Choke Cherry Road
Rockville, MD 20857
(877) 726-4727
Website: http://www.samhsa.gov

Part of U.S. Department of Health and Human Services, SAMHSA is a federal agency that researches and provides information on a wide variety of mental health issues. SAMHSA publications cover things like domestic abuse, trauma, and depression, as well as substance abuse.

WEBSITES

Because of the changing nature of Internet links, Rosen Publishing has developed an online list of websites related to the subject of this book. This site is updated regularly. Please use this link to access the list:

http://www.rosenlinks.com/411/Alco

FOR FURTHER READING

Black, Claudia. *It Will Never Happen to Me!* New York, NY: Ballantine/Random House, 1987.

Bryfonski, Dedria, ed. *Family Violence.* Farmington Hills, MI: Greenhaven Press, 2013.

Centre for Addiction and Mental Health. *Wishes and Worries: Coping with a Parent Who Drinks Too Much Alcohol.* Toronto, ON, Canada: Tundra Books, 2011.

Crist, James J. *Mad: How to Deal with Your Anger and Get Respect.* Minneapolis, MN: Free Spirit Publishing, 2008.

Desetta, Al, ed. *Pressure: True Stories by Teens About Stress.* Minneapolis, MN: Free Spirit Publishing, 2012.

Duhigg, Charles. *The Power of Habit: Why We Do What We Do in Life and Business.* New York, NY: Random House, 2012.

Espejo, Roman. *Chemical Dependency.* Detroit, MI: Greenhaven Press, 2011.

Fisanick, Christina. *Addiction: Opposing Viewpoints.* Detroit, MI: Greenhaven Press, 2009.

Fox, Marci, and Leslie Sokol. *Think Confident, Be Confident for Teens: A Cognitive Therapy Guide to Overcoming Self-Doubt and Creating*

Unshakable Self-Esteem. Oakland, CA: New
Harbinger Publications, 2011.

Gordon, Sherri Mabry. *Beyond Bruises: The Truth
About Teens and Abuse.* Berkeley Heights, NJ:
Enslow Publishers, 2009.

Haroutunian, Harry. *Being Sober.* New York, NY:
Rodale, 2013.

Haugen, David M. *Addiction.* Detroit, MI:
Greenhaven Press, 2013.

Hipp, Earl. *Fighting Invisible Tigers: Stress Management
for Teens.* 3rd ed. Minneapolis, MN: Free Spirit
Publishing, 2008.

Jones, Jami L. *Bouncing Back: Dealing with the
Stuff Life Throws at You.* New York, NY:
Franklin Watts/Scholastic, 2007.

Kinsey, Brian. *Substance Abuse, Addiction, and Treatment.*
Tarrytown, NY: Marshall Cavendish, 2012.

Lawford, Christopher Kennedy. *Moments of Clarity:
Voices from the Front Lines of Addiction and
Recovery.* New York, NY: HarperCollins, 2009.

Lawford, Christopher Kennedy. *What Addicts
Know: 10 Lessons from Recovery to Benefit
Everyone.* Dallas, TX: BenBella Books, 2014.

Longhine, Laura, ed. *Rage: True Stories by Teens
About Anger.* Minneapolis, MN: Free Spirit
Publishing, 2012.

Lucas, Eileen. *More Than the Blues? Understanding
and Dealing with Depression.* Berkeley Heights,
NJ: Enslow Publishers, 2009.

Parks, Peggy. *Teen Depression*. Farmington Hills, MI: Lucent Books, 2012.

Reed, Amy Lynn. *Clean*. New York, NY: Simon Pulse, 2012.

Schab, Lisa M. *The Anxiety Workbook for Teens: Activities to Help You Deal with Anxiety and Worry*. Oakland, CA: New Harbinger Publications, 2008.

Shantz-Hilkes, Chloe, ed. *Hooked: When Addiction Hits Home*. Toronto, ON, Canada: Annick Press, 2013.

Simons, Rae. *Survival Skills: How to Handle Life's Catastrophes*. Broomall, PA: Mason Crest Publishers, 2009.

Thorne, Melanie. *Hand Me Down*. New York, NY: Dutton, 2012.

BIBLIOGRAPHY

Adult Children of Alcoholics World Service Organization, Inc. "The Laundry List." Retrieved January 20, 2014 (http://www.adultchildren .org/lit/Laundry_List.php).

Adult Children of Alcoholics World Service Organization, Inc. "The Problem." Retrieved January 20, 2014 (http://www.adultchildren .org/lit/Problem.s).

Branson, Mary (licensed professional counselor and licensed marriage and family therapist) in discussion with the author, January 2014.

Cartwright, Michael. *Believable Hope: Five Essential Elements to Beat Any Addiction.* Deerfield Beach, FL: Health Communications, Inc., 2012.

Center for Behavioral Health Statistics and Quality (U.S. Department of Health and Human Services). "Results from the 2012 National Survey on Drug Use and Health: Summary of National Findings." Retrieved January 10, 2014 (http://www.samhsa.gov/ data/NSDUH/2012SummNatFindDetTables/ index.aspx).

Centers for Disease Control and Prevention. "Fact Sheets—Alcohol Use and Health." Retrieved December 5, 2013 (http://www.cdc.gov/alcohol/fact-sheets/alcohol-use.htm).

"Coping with an Alcoholic Parent." Sherborn, MA: Aquarius Health Care Media, 2006, video.

Dayton, Tian. "Portrait of an Alcoholic Family." *Huffington Post,* February 16, 2010. Retrieved January 28, 2014 (http://www.huffingtonpost.com/dr-tian-dayton/portrait-of-an-alcoholic_b_463876.html).

Downs, Martin. "Challenging Old Assumptions About Alcoholism." NYTimes.com. Retrieved January 10, 2014 (http://www.nytimes.com/ref/health/healthguide/esn-alcoholism).

Downs, Martin. "What to Ask About Alcoholism?" NYTimes.com. Retrieved January 12, 2014 (http://www.nytimes.com/ref/health/healthguide/esn-alcoholism).

Eskapa, Roy. *The Cure for Alcoholism: The Medically Proven Way to Eliminate Alcohol Addiction.* Dallas, TX: BenBella Books, 2012.

Fletcher, Anne M. *Inside Rehab.* New York, NY: Viking, 2013.

Glaser, Gabrielle. "Cold Turkey Isn't the Only Route." *New York Times*, January 2, 2014.

Hoffman, John, and Susan Froemke, eds. *Addiction: Why Can't They Just Stop?* New York, NY: Rodale, 2007.

Hunnicutt, Susan, ed. *Interventions.* Farmington Hills, MI: Gale/Cengage Learning, 2012.

Jay, Jeff, and Debra Jay. *Love First: A Family's Guide to Intervention.* Center City, MN: Hazelden, 2008.

Lawford, Christopher Kennedy. *Recover to Live: Kick Any Habit, Manage Any Addiction.* Dallas, TX: BenBella Books, 2013.

National Council on Alcoholism and Drug Dependence, Inc. "Am I Alcoholic?" Retrieved February 7, 2014 (http://www.ncadd.org/index.php/learn-about-alcohol/alcohol-abuse-self-test).

National Institute on Alcohol Abuse and Alcoholism. "Module 10J: Alcohol and the Family." Retrieved January 11, 2014 (http://pubs.niaaa.nih.gov/publications/Social/Module10JFamilies/Module10J.html).

Perkins, Cynthia. "Understanding Alcohol Addiction." Retrieved February 2, 2014 (http://www.alternatives-for-alcoholism.com/alcohol-addiction.html).

Research Society on Alcoholism. "Impact of Alcoholism and Alcohol Induced Disease on America." April 20, 2011. Retrieved December 18, 2013 (http://www.rsoa.org/2011-04-11RSAWhitePaper.pdf).

Schwartz, Jeffrey M., and Rebecca Gladding. *You Are Not Your Brain.* New York, NY: Avery/Penguin, 2011.

Substance Abuse and Mental Health Services Administration Center for Substance Abuse Treatment. "Enhancing Motivation for Change in Substance Abuse Treatment." Rockville, MD: HHS Publication No. (SMA) 13-4212. Retrieved February 4, 2014 (http://store.samhsa.gov/shin/content//SMA13-4212/SMA13-4212.pdf).

Substance Abuse and Mental Health Services Administration Center for Substance Abuse Treatment. "Families Are the Frontline: Preventing, Treating, and Recovering from Substance Use and Mental Disorders." Retrieved January 20, 2014 (http://store.samhas.gov/product).

Substance Abuse and Mental Health Services Administration Center for Substance Abuse Treatment. "Recovery Is a Family Affair: The Complex Dynamics in Families Struggling with Mental and Substance Use Disorders." Retrieved January 21, 2014 (http://store.samhas.gov/product).

Substance Abuse and Mental Health Services Administration Center for Substance Abuse Treatment. "What Is Substance Abuse Treatment? A Booklet for Families." 75th printing. Retrieved February 5, 2014 (http://store.samhsa.gov/shin/content//SMA08-4126/SMA08-4126.pdf).

Twelve Steps and Twelve Traditions. New York, NY: Alcoholics Anonymous World Services, Inc., 2011.

Urschel III, Harold C. *Healing the Addicted Brain: The Revolutionary, Science-Based Alcoholism and Addiction Recovery Program.* Naperville, IL: Sourcebooks, Inc., 2009.

Watkins, Christine, ed. *Alcohol Abuse.* Farmington Hills, MI: Gale/Cengage Learning, 2012.

INDEX

A

acamprosate, 78
Adult Children of
    Alcoholics World Service
    Organization, Inc.,
    46–48, 92
Al-Anon, 58–59, 89
Alateen, 57, 58–59, 89
alcohol
    abstinence from, 76
    amounts of in one drink, 10
    building tolerance to,
        15, 31
    people who shouldn't drink,
        11–13
Alcoholics Anonymous, 38,
    58–59, 63, 75–76, 82
alcoholism
    as a disease, 30, 76, 83, 88
    causes of, 23–34
    coping with a parent's,
        49–61
    effect on family, 6, 7, 16–18,
        20–21, 26, 35–48, 49–51,
        91–92
    family history of, 23–25,
        35, 46
    myths and facts about, 22
    problems related to, 6, 8,
        15, 45
    recognizing, 8–21
    self-test for, 14–15

statistics on, 4–6
symptoms/signs of, 13–15

B

barbiturates, 66
behavior, effects of alcohol on,
    18–19
Beyond Rehab, 67
binge drinking, defined, 11
Black, Claudia, 37, 48
brain chemistry, changes in,
    31, 33–34, 35
Branson, Mary, 21, 30, 38–39
"bumper stickers," 79–81

C

Centers for Disease Control
    and Prevention (CDC),
    10–11
Center for Substance Abuse
    Treatment (CSAT), 66
children, lasting effects of
    parent's alcoholism on,
    46–48, 51
cocaine, 31, 66
cognitive therapy, 79–81
cold turkey, going, 66
co-occurring disorders, 30
"Coping with an Alcoholic
    Parent," 23–25, 91
counseling, 15, 38, 48, 56, 57,
    62, 67, 73–75

About the Author

Writer and educator Terry Teague Meyer lives in Houston, Texas. She has taught at the middle school, high school, and college levels and mentored at the elementary level. She has written several nonfiction books for young people, including books on character development and adapting to difficult situations.

Photo Credits

Cover, pp. 1, 24 Creatista/Shutterstock.com; pp. 4–5, 16–17 ejwhite/Shutterstock.com; pp. 8–9 stephenkirsh/Shutterstock .com; p. 12 Stefanie Sudek/Stock4B/Getty Images; p. 20 kristian sekulic/Vetta/Getty Images; pp. 26–27 Randy Faris/ Fuse/Thinkstock; pp. 28–29 altrendo images/Getty Images; pp. 32–33 Zero Creatives/Image Source/Getty Images; pp. 36–37 wavebreakmedia/Shutterstock.com; pp. 38–39, 60–61 monkeybusinessimages/iStock/Thinkstock; pp. 40–41 Michael Blann/Digital Vision/Thinkstock; p. 43 Pixland/ Thinkstock; p. 47 Monkey Business Images/Shutterstock. com; p. 50 SW Productions/Photodisc/Getty Images; p. 53 Design Pics/Hanson Ng/Getty Images; pp. 54–55 Nancy Ney/ Photodisc/Getty Images; pp. 64–65 Alina Solovyova-Vincent/ E+/Getty Images; p. 68 Tim Chapman/Hulton Archive/ Getty Images; pp. 70–71 Flying Colors Ltd/Photodisc/Getty Images; pp. 74–75 Catherine Yeulet/iStock/Thinkstock; p. 80 David Livingston/Getty Images; pp. 84–85 ambrozinio/ Shutterstock.com; pp. 86–87 ronstik/Shutterstock.com; pp. 90–91 © iStockphoto.com/Steve Debenport.

Designer: Les Kanturek; Editor: Tracey Baptiste;
Photo Researcher: Karen Huang